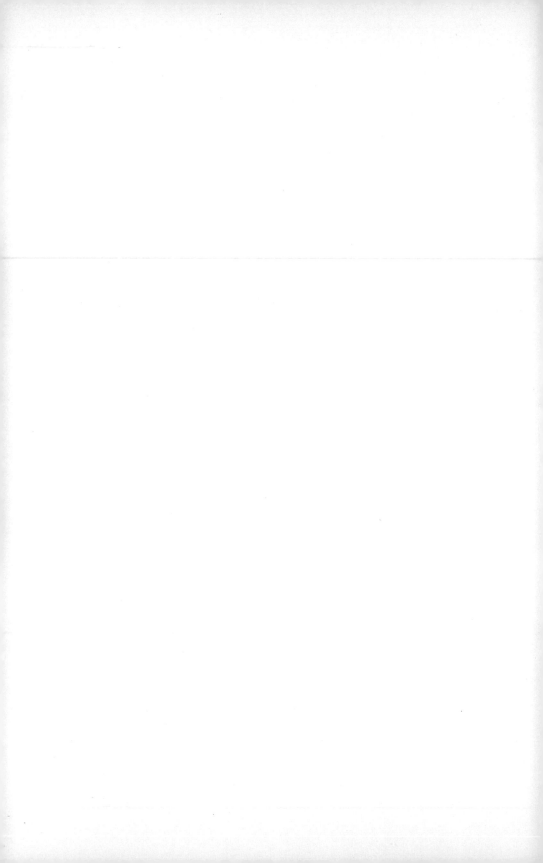

HAN ON THE RUN

Written by Beth Davies

Penguin
Random
House

Editor Beth Davies
Designer Chris Gould
Senior Pre-production Producer Jennifer Murray
Senior Producer Mary Slater
Managing Editor Sadie Smith
Managing Art Editor Vicky Short
Publisher Julie Ferris
Art Director Lisa Lanzarini
Publishing Director Simon Beecroft

For Lucasfilm
Editor Samantha Holland
Creative Director of Publishing Michael Siglain
Art Director Troy Alders
Story Group James Waugh, Pablo Hidalgo,
and Leland Chee
Asset Group Steve Newman, Newell Todd,
Gabrielle Levenson, Erik Sanchez, and Bryce Pinkos
Photographers Jonathan Olley, John Wilson, Ed Miller,
and Shannon Kirbie

First American Edition, 2018
Published in the United States by DK Publishing
345 Hudson Street, New York, New York 10014

Page design copyright © 2018 Dorling Kindersley Limited
DK, a Division of Penguin Random House LLC
18 19 20 21 22 10 9 8 7 6 5 4 3 2 1
001–305885–May/2018

A catalog record for this book is available from the Library of Congress.

ISBN: 978-1-4654-6687-7 (Paperback)
ISBN: 978-1-4654-6688-4 (Hardcover)

DK books are available at special discounts when purchased in bulk for
sales promotions, premiums, fund-raising, or educational use.
For details, contact: DK Publishing Special Markets,
345 Hudson Street, New York, New York 10014
SpecialSales@dk.com

Printed and bound in China

A WORLD OF IDEAS:
SEE ALL THERE IS TO KNOW

www.dk.com
www.starwars.com

Contents

Young Han

Meet Han Solo. Brave Han is a quick thinker, but his plans often get him into trouble.

Han was born on a planet called Corellia. He wants to leave his home and see the galaxy.

Visitors to Corellia travel through the Coronet Spaceport.

A gang of criminals called the White Worms also live on Corellia. The White Worms make others carry out their crimes for them.

Han loses some valuable hyperspace fuel that belongs to the White Worms. Han runs away from the angry White Worms. He keeps a small bit of fuel for himself.

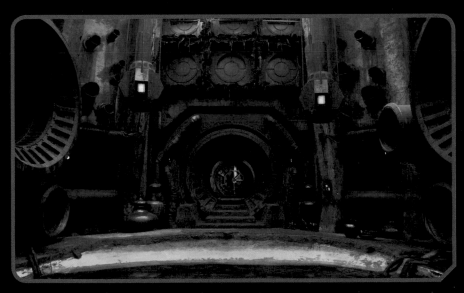

The White Worms live underground, out of the sunlight.

Han has to get away from Corellia quickly. The White Worms order their scrumrat workers to find him. Rebolt also works for the White Worms. He chases after Han with some angry hounds.

Scrumrats

Rebolt

Corellian hounds

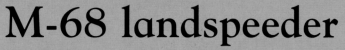

M-68 landspeeder

Han has an M-68 landspeeder. He uses it to escape from the White Worms.

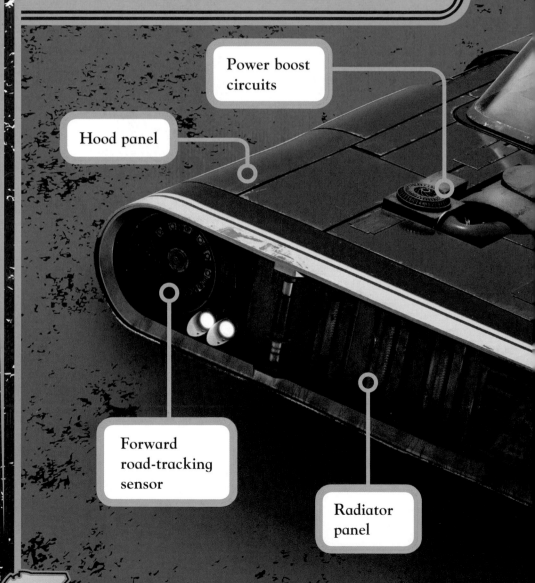

Power boost circuits

Hood panel

Forward road-tracking sensor

Radiator panel

Spoiler to reduce drag

Driver's seat

Turbine engine

Repulsorlift power regulator

Qi'ra is Han's best friend on Corellia. She is the only person that he trusts to be his copilot. They sometimes argue about the quickest routes through the streets. Han and Qi'ra try to run away together, but they get separated at the spaceport.

Loyal Han gives Qi'ra his lucky pair of gold dice when the friends are separated.

Imperial life

The Empire controls Corellia, along with most of the galaxy. It builds huge starships in Corellia's factories.

The Empire's patrol troopers keep order on the streets. They look out for troublemakers like Han!

Patrol troopers travel on narrow patrol speeder bikes.

The only way for Han to leave
Corellia is to join the Empire.
Han wants to be a pilot, but is
made to work as a mudtrooper.
   Mudtroopers fight for the Empire
on a muddy planet called Mimban.
The Empire is fighting the brave
local forces who live there.

Mimbanese
soldier

Imperial forces

During his adventures, Han runs into many different Imperial soldiers. They all have different jobs.

Patrol trooper
Patrol troopers mainly deal with street crime. They ride fast speeders through cities.

Mudtrooper
Mudtroopers fight in muddy fields. They wear dark clothing and carry simple weapons.

Stormtrooper
Stormtroopers work all over the galaxy. This one is dirty after fighting on Mimban.

Range trooper
These troopers work on a cold planet with high mountains. They are very strong and tough.

Imperial officer
Imperial bases are run by officers. They wear smart uniforms with not much armor.

Han gets into trouble with an Imperial officer and gets locked in a prison cell. He meets a muddy creature known as "the Beast." The Beast's real name is Chewbacca. He is a Wookiee.

Chewbacca has lost his family. He hopes to find them again one day. Chewbacca is very loyal, but can be grumpy!

Wookiees have long, thick coats of hair.

Han also meets a man named Beckett. Beckett is disguised as an Imperial officer, but he is really a criminal.

AT-hauler

Beckett and his friends plan to steal an Imperial vehicle called an AT-hauler. Beckett uses the hauler to help Han and Chewbacca escape from the Empire. Beckett invites the pair to join his crew.

Vandor is a rocky planet with lots of mountains.

Thief!

Beckett's gang is planning a big robbery! The Empire is transporting valuable fuel across a planet called Vandor.

The gang wants to steal the fuel from a fast-moving vehicle called a conveyex. It travels on very high tracks.

Beckett's crew are very skilled.
Val is an expert with technology.
She will stop the
vehicle on
the tracks.

Range troopers wear special boots to help them stand on the conveyex.

The gang will use the stolen AT-hauler to pick up the fuel. Imperial soldiers called range troopers stand on the conveyex and guard the fuel inside. Watch out, gang!

Beckett's crew are not the only thieves on Vandor. Enfys Nest is the leader of a gang called the Cloud-Riders. Enfys also wants to steal the fuel.

The Cloud-Riders all wear masks and travel on very fast swoop bikes. Each bike looks different.

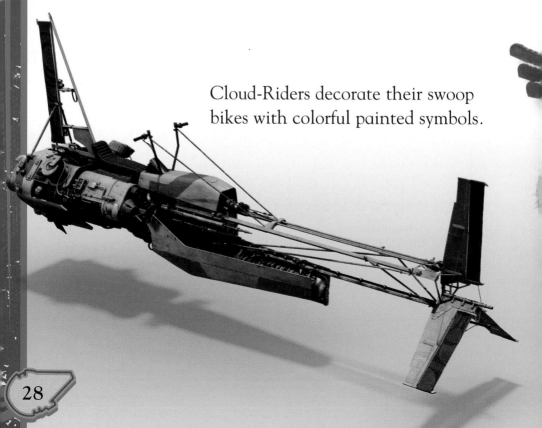

Cloud-Riders decorate their swoop bikes with colorful painted symbols.

Food from around the galaxy is served on the yacht.

Beckett has promised the fuel to a criminal group called the Crimson Dawn. The fuel is destroyed in an accident. Now, Han has to think of a new plan to get the fuel.

The crew visit a grand star yacht to meet with the Crimson Dawn. They are greeted by a droid who takes their weapons away.

The Crimson Dawn employs many dangerous aliens. An alien named Aemon leads a group of guards who work aboard the yacht.

Aemon

Yacht guard

Qi'ra also works for the Crimson Dawn. Han is surprised to meet Qi'ra again after all these years. Can he still trust his old friend?

Qi'ra

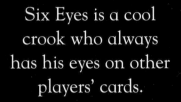

Six Eyes is a cool crook who always has his eyes on other players' cards.

This one-eyed player is named Glaucus. His big coat hides his body and his playing cards.

The Lodge

Qi'ra takes Han and the gang to the Lodge. The Lodge is a place visitors come to eat, drink, and play cards. Maybe someone here can help Han with a new plan.

Two heads are better than one for the Twins. Their two heads are joined to one body!

Therm Scissorpunch is looking to snap up prizes, but he might take your fingers, too.

Dava Cassamam rarely leaves the card table. A huge dome covers her head.

Ace pilot

Han has a new plan to
get the fuel. He will fly
to a planet called Kessel,
where the fuel is mined.

Han is a very good pilot,
but he needs a fast ship.
Han makes a deal to
use one called the
Millennium Falcon.
The ship is owned
and piloted by
a man named
Lando Calrissian.

Lando loves the
Millennium Falcon
and does not want
Han to damage it.

Lando works with a droid named L3-37. She has the best navigation system in the galaxy.

Droids control the mines' computer systems.

A criminal gang called the
Pyke Syndicate runs the mines
on Kessel. The mines are
covered in thick orange dust.
There are many other workers
in the mines, including droids.
There are also a lot of Wookiees
like Chewbacca. They help Han's
gang escape with the fuel.

The fuel is very dangerous. It must be kept at the right temperature or it will explode! Han must quickly and safely transport the fuel away from Kessel. He will have to use all of his skills as a pilot. Good luck, Han!

Fuel
container

Quiz

1. Who has the best navigation system in the galaxy?

2. Where was Han born?

3. What is Chewbacca's nickname on Mimban?

4. Which member of Beckett's gang is an expert with technology?

5. Who is the leader of the Cloud-Riders?

6. What item does Han give to Qi'ra?

7. Which group does Beckett promise the fuel to?

8. What is the name of Lando's starship?

9. True or false:
   The White Worms
   run the Kessel mines.

10. Which planet is
    the Lodge on?

Answers
on page 47.

Glossary

Empire
The evil organization that controls the galaxy

hyperspace
An area of space where starships travel at top speeds

Imperial
Part of the Empire

navigation system
A machine that helps plan the best way
to reach a destination

scrumat
Children and teenagers who work for the White
Worms gang

spaceport
A place where starships and people can leave
or arrive on a planet

Wookiee
A hairy being from the planet Kashyyyk

yacht
A large, expensive vehicle

Index

Answers to the quiz on pages 44 and 45:
1. L3-37 2. Corellia 3. The Beast 4. Val 5. Enfys Nest 6. A pair
of gold dice 7. The Crimson Dawn 8. The *Millennium Falcon*
9. False—the Pyke Syndicate runs the mines. 10. Vandor

A LEVEL FOR EVERY READER

This book is a part of an exciting four-level reading series to support children in developing the habit of reading widely for both pleasure and information. Each book is designed to develop a child's reading skills, fluency, grammar awareness, and comprehension in order to build confidence and enjoyment when reading.

Ready for a Level 2 (Beginning to Read) book
A child should:
- be able to recognize a bank of common words quickly and be able to blend sounds together to make some words.
- be familiar with using beginner letter sounds and context clues to figure out unfamiliar words.
- sometimes correct his/her reading if it doesn't look right or make sense.
- be aware of the need for a slight pause at commas and a longer one at periods.

A valuable and shared reading experience
For many children, reading requires much effort, but adult participation can make reading both fun and easier. Here are a few tips on how to use this book with a young reader:

Check out the contents together:
- read about the book on the back cover and talk about the contents page to help heighten interest and expectation.
- discuss new or difficult words.
- chat about labels, annotations, and pictures.

Support the reader:
- give the book to the young reader to turn the pages.
- where necessary, encourage longer words to be broken into syllables, sound out each one, and then flow the syllables together; ask him/her to reread the sentence to check the meaning.
- encourage the reader to vary her/his voice as she/he reads; demonstrate how to do this if helpful.

Talk at the end of each book, or after every few pages:
- ask questions about the text and the meaning of the words used—this helps develop comprehension skills.
- read the quiz at the end of the book and encourage the reader to answer the questions, if necessary, by turning back to the relevant pages to find the answers.